A Bouquet of Poems and Roses

A Celebration of Love in Flowers and Verse

Edited by J. S. Roberts

BARNES
&NOBLE
BOOKS
NEW YORK

Rosa Pomponia

To the Reader

Known as the "Raphael of flowers," Pierre-Joseph Redouté (1759-1840) was a gifted naturalist and painter. His eye captured not only the details of each bloom, but also its grace and bearing, the essence of its fragile beauty. His talents in botany and art earned him patronage at the courts of the three regimes that ruled France in his lifetime. One of his crowning achievements was the commission by the Empress Josephine to paint the magnificent roses of the gardens in her retreat, Malmaison. We have chosen the most beautiful of these roses to illustrate this book.

Redouté's evocations of nature's beauty are as timeless as the poets' expressions of love that we have included here. Shakespeare knew "That in black ink my love shall still shine bright," for thoughts of love, when true, never tarnish.

We offer to you then, this bouquet of roses and verse. They pay homage to our love of beauty, and to the beauty of love.

✑ *J.S.R.*

Rosa alba foliacea

Song 1st by a Shepherd

Welcome, stranger, to this place,
Where joy doth sit on every bough,
Paleness flies from every face;
We reap not what we do not sow.

Innocence doth like a Rose,
Bloom on every Maiden's cheek;
Honor twines around her brows,
The jewel Health adorns her neck.

❧ *William Blake*

A Match

If love were what the rose is,
　And I were like the leaf,
Our lives would grow together
In sad or singing weather,
Blown fields or flowerful closes,
　Green pleasure or gray grief;
If love were what the rose is,
　And I were like the leaf.

If you were April's lady,
　And I were lord in May,
We'd throw with leaves for hours
And draw for days with flowers,
Till day like night were shady
　And night were bright like day;
If you were April's lady,
　And I were lord in May.

ᴥ *ALGERNON CHARLES SWINBURNE*

Rosa Indica vulgaris

Rosa Damascena subalba

Gather Ye Roses

Gather ye roses while ye may,
  Old time is still a-flying;
A world where beauty fleets away
  Is no world for denying.
Come lads and lasses, fall to play
  Lose no more time in sighing.

The very flowers you pluck to-day
  To-morrow will be dying;
  And all the flowers are crying,
And all the leaves have tongues to say,—
Gather ye roses while ye may.

Robert Louis Stevenson

The Lover Tells of the Rose in His Heart

All things uncomely and broken, all things worn out
and old.
The cry of a child by the roadway, the creak of a
lumbering cart,
The heavy steps of the ploughman, splashing the
wintry mould,
Are wronging your image that blossoms a rose in the
deeps of my heart.

The wrong of unshapely things is a wrong too great to
be told;
I hunger to build them anew and sit on a green knoll
apart,
With the earth and the sky and the water, remade, like
a casket of gold
For my dreams of your image that blossoms a rose in
the deeps of my heart.

ও *WILLIAM BUTLER YEATS*

Rosa Gallica rosea flore simplici

Rosa Gallica Versicolor

FROM

The Green Linnet

Beneath these fruit-tree boughs that shed
Their snow-white blossoms on my head,
With brightest sunshine round me spread
    Of spring's unclouded weather,
In this sequestered nook how sweet
To sit upon my orchard-seat!
And birds and flowers once more to greet,
    My last year's friends together.

One have I marked, the happiest guest
In all this covert of the blest:
Hail to Thee, far above the rest
    In joy of voice and pinion!
Thou, Linnet! in thy green array,
Presiding Spirit here to-day,
Dost lead the revels of the May;
    And this is thy dominion.

⁖ *WILLIAM WORDSWORTH*

To a Skylark

Hail to thee, blithe Spirit!
   Bird thou never wert,
That from Heaven, or near it,
   Pourest thy full heart
In profuse strains of unpremeditated art.

Like a rose embowered
   In its own green leaves,
By warm winds deflowered,
   Till the scent it gives
Makes faint with too much sweet these
   heavy-winged thieves.

✑ *PERCY BYSSHE SHELLEY*

Rosa Muscosa Anemone-flora

Rosa Damascena Italica

FROM

A Contemplation Upon Flowers

Brave flowers, that I could gallant it like you,
And be as little vain;
You come abroad and make a harmless show,
And to your beds of earth again;
You are not proud, you know your birth,
For your embroidered garments are from earth.

You do obey your months and times, but I
Would have it ever spring;
My fate would know no winter, never die,
Nor think of such a thing;
Oh that I could my bed of earth but view,
And smile and look as cheerfully as you.

၍ *HENRY KING*

Song

Love and harmony combine,
And around our souls intwine,
While thy branches mix with mine,
And our roots together join.

Joys upon our branches sit,
Chirping loud, and singing sweet;
Like gentle streams beneath our feet
Innocence and virtue meet.

Thou the golden fruit dost bear,
I am clad in flowers fair;
Thy sweet boughs perfume the air,
And the turtle buildeth there.

 WILLIAM BLAKE

Rosa Lucida

Rosa Indica fragrans

FROM

All That's Past

Very old are the woods;
    And the buds that break
Out of the briar's boughs,
    When March winds wake,
So old with their beauty are—
    Oh, no man knows
Through what wild centuries
    Roves back the rose.

Very old are the brooks;
    And the rills that rise
Where snows sleep cold beneath
    The azure skies
Sing such a history
    Of come and gone,
Their every drop is as wise
    As Solomon.

ᔥ *WALTER DE LA MARE*

FROM

I Wandered Lonely as a Cloud

I wandered lonely as a cloud
That floats on high o'er vales and hills,
When all at once I saw a crowd,
A host of golden daffodils,
Beside the lake, beneath the trees
Fluttering and dancing in the breeze.

For oft, when on my couch I lie
In vacant or in pensive mood,
They flash upon that inward eye
Which is the bliss of solitude;
And then my heart with pleasure fills,
And dances with the daffodils.

✌ *WILLIAM WORDSWORTH*

Rosa muscosa multiplex

Rosa Brevistyla Leucochroa

Green Rain

Into the scented woods we'll go,
And see the blackthorn swim in snow.
High above, in the budding leaves,
A brooding dove awakes and grieves;
The glades with mingled music stir,
And wildly laughs the woodpecker.
When blackthorn petals pearl the breeze,
There are the twisted hawthorne trees
Thick-set with buds, as clear and pale
As golden water or green hail—
As if a storm of rain had stood
Enchanted in the thorny wood,
And, hearing fairy voices call,
Hung poised, forgetting how to fall.

❧ *Mary Webb*

For Miriam

The sea is awash with roses O they blow
Upon the land

The still hills fill with their scent
O the hills flow on their sweetness
As on God's hand

O love, it is so little we know of pleasure
Pleasure that lasts as the snow

But the sea is awash with roses O they blow
Upon the land

KENNETH PATCHEN

Rosa Moschata flore semi-pleno

Rosa Damascena Coccinea

FROM

To Althea, from Prison

Stone walls do not a prison make,
    Nor iron bars a cage;
Minds innocent and quiet take
    That for an hermitage;
If I have freedom in my love
    And in my soul am free,
Angels alone, that soar above,
    Enjoy such liberty.

 RICHARD LOVELACE

Song

What is there hid in the heart of a rose,
        Mother-mine?
Ah, who knows, who knows, who knows?
A Man that died on a lonely hill
May tell you, perhaps, but none other will,
        Little child.

What does it take to make a rose,
        Mother-mine?
The God that died to make it knows
It takes the world's eternal wars,
It takes the moon and all the stars
It takes the might of heaven and hell
And the everlasting Love as well,
        Little child.

ALFRED NOYES

Rosa centifolia Bullata

Rosa alba Regalis

It Was the Time of Roses

It was not in the winter
Our loving lot was cast:
It was the time of roses—
We plucked them as we passed!

That churlish season never frowned
On early lovers yet!
O, no—the world was newly crowned
With flowers, when first we met.

'Twas twilight, and I bade you go,
But still you held me fast:
It was the time of roses—
We plucked them as we passed. . . .

THOMAS HOOD

The Noble Nature

It is not growing like a tree
    In bulk, doth make man better be;
Or standing long an oak, three hundred year,
To fall a log at last, dry, bald, and sear:
    A lily of a day
    Is fairer far in May,
  Although it fall and die that night,—
  It was the plant and flower of Light.
In small proportions we just beauties see,
And in short measures life may perfect be.

✑ BEN JONSON

Rosa Rubrifolia

Rosa Indica Cruenta

The Passionate Shepherd to His Love

Come live with me and be my Love,
And we will all the pleasures prove
That hills and valleys, dales and fields,
Or woods or steep mountain yields.

And we will sit upon the rocks,
And see the shepherds feed their flocks
By shallow rivers, to whose falls
Melodious birds sing madrigals.

And I will make thee beds of roses
And a thousand fragrant posies;
A cap of flowers, and a kirtle
Embroider'd all with leaves of myrtle.

A gown made of the finest wool
Which from our pretty lambs we pull;
Fair-lined slippers for the cold,
With buckles of the purest gold.

A belt of straw and ivy-buds
With coral clasps and amber studs:
And if these pleasures may thee move,
Come live with me and be my Love.

CHRISTOPHER MARLOWE

FROM

The Garden

What wondrous life is this I lead!
Ripe apples drop about my head;
The luscious clusters of the vine
Upon my mouth do crush their wine;
The nectarine and curious peach
Into my hands themselves do reach;
Stumbling on melons, as I pass,
Insnared with flowers, I fall on grass.

How well the skillful gardener drew
Of flowers and herbs this dial new,
Where, from above, the milder sun
Does through a fragrant zodiac run;
And as it works th' industrious bee
Computes its time as well as we!
How could such sweet and wholesome hours
Be reckoned but with herbs and flowers?

❧ *ANDREW MARVELL*

Rosa Eglanteria

Rosa Indica

I Remember

I remember, I remember,
The roses, red and white,
The violets, and the lily-cups!—
Those flowers made of light!
The lilacs where the robin built,
And where my brother set
The laburnum on his birth-day,—
The tree is living yet!

I remember, I remember,
The fir trees dark and high;
I used to think their slender tops
Were close against the sky:
It was a childish ignorance,
But now 'tis little joy
To know I'm farther off from Heaven
Than when I was a boy.

❧ *THOMAS HOOD*

Song of Songs

I am the rose of Sharon,
And the lily of the valleys.
As the lily among thorns,
So is my love among the daughters.
As the apple tree among the trees of the wood,
So is my beloved among the sons.

✑ *THE BIBLE*

Rosa Nivea

Rosa Pimpinellifolia flore variegato

The Mystery

He came and took me by the hand
    Up to a red rose tree,
He kept His meaning to Himself
    But gave a rose to me.
I did not pray Him to lay bare
    The mystery to me,
Enough the rose was Heaven to smell,
And His own face to see.

❧ *RALPH HODGSON*

FROM

Song

Love laid his sleepless head
On a thorny rosy bed;
And his eyes with tears were red,
And pale his lips as the dead.

And Joy came up with the day,
And kissed Love's lips as he lay,
And the watchers ghostly and gray
Sped from his pillow away.

And his eyes as the dawn grew bright,
And his lips waxed ruddy as light:
Sorrow may reign for a night,
But day shall bring back delight.

✌ *ALGERNON CHARLES SWINBURNE*

Rosa Pumila

Rosa Gallica Pontiana

It was a Lover

It was a Lover, and his lasse,
    With a hey, and a ho, and a hey nonino,
That ore the greene corne-field did passe,
    In spring time, the onely pretty ring time,
When Birds do sing, *hey ding a ding, ding:*
Sweet Lovers love the spring.

Between the acres of the Rie,
    With a hey, and a ho, and a hey nonino,
These prettie Country folks would lie,
    In spring time, the onely pretty ring time,
When Birds do sing, *hey ding a ding, ding:*
Sweet Lovers love the spring.

This Carroll they began that houre,
    With a hey, and a ho, and a hey nonino,
How that a life was but a Flower,
    In spring time, the onely pretty ring time,
When Birds do sing, *hey ding a ding, ding:*
Sweet Lovers love the spring.

And therefore take the present time,
    With a hey, and a ho, and a hey nonino,
For love is crowned with the prime
    In spring time, the onely pretty ring time,
When Birds do sing, *hey ding a ding, ding:*
Sweet Lovers love the spring.

∾ *WILLIAM SHAKESPEARE*

Rosy Apple, Lemon or Pear

Rosy apple, lemon or pear,
Bunch of roses she shall wear;
Gold and silver by her side,
I know who will be the bride.
Take her by her lily-white hand,
    Lead her to the altar;
Give her kisses,—one, two, three,—
    Mother's runaway daughter.

❦ *Anonymous*

Rosa Indica fragrans flore simplici

Rosa Gallica Granatus

Sonnet XVIII

Shall I compare thee to a Summer's day?
Thou art more lovely and more temperate:
Rough winds do shake the darling buds of May,
And Summer's lease hath all too short a date:
Sometime too hot the eye of heaven shines,
And often is his gold complexion dimm'd;
And every fair from fair sometime declines,
By chance or nature's changing course untrimm'd;
But the eternal summer shall not fade,
Nor lose possession of that fair thou ow'st;
Nor shall Death brag thou wander'st in his shade,
When in eternal lines to time thou grow'st:
    So long as men can breathe, or eyes can see,
    So long lives this, and this gives life to thee.

WILLIAM SHAKESPEARE

The Question

I dreamed that, as I wandered by the way,
    Bare Winter suddenly was changed to Spring,
And gentle odours led my steps astray,
    Mixed with a sound of waters murmuring
Along a shelving bank of turf, which lay
    Under a copse, and hardly dared to fling
Its green arms round the bosom of the stream,
But kissed it and then fled, as thou mightest in dream.

And in the warm hedge grew lush eglantine,
    Green cowbind and the moonlight-coloured may
And cherry-blossoms, and white cups, whose wine
    Was the bright dew, yet drained not by the day;
And wild roses, and ivy serpentine
    With its dark buds and leaves, wandering astray;
And flowers azure, black, and streaked with gold,
Fairer than any wakened eyes behold.

Methought that of these visionary flowers
    I made a nosegay, bound in such a way
That the same hues, which in their natural bowers
    Were mingled or opposed, the like array
Kept these imprisoned children of the Hours
    Within my hand,—and then, elate and gay,
I hastened to the spot whence I had come,
That I might there present it!—Oh! to whom?

PERCY BYSSHE SHELLEY

Rosa Gallica Aurelianensis

Rosa l'heritieranea

Loveliest of Trees,
the Cherry Now

Loveliest of trees, the cherry now
Is hung with bloom along the bough,
And stands about the woodland ride
Wearing white for Eastertide.

Now, of my threescore years and ten,
Twenty will not come again,
And take from seventy springs a score,
It only leaves me fifty more.

And since to look at things in bloom
Fifty springs are little room,
About the woodlands I will go
To see the cherry hung with snow.

ও *A.E. Housman*

FROM

A Birthday

My heart is like a singing bird
    Whose nest is in a watered shoot;
My heart is like an apple-tree
    Whose boughs are bent with thick-set fruit;
My heart is like a rainbow shell
    That paddles in a halcyon sea;
My heart is gladder than all these
    Because my love is come to me.

∾ *CHRISTINA ROSSETTI*

Rosa Gallica

Rosa Gallica latifolia

My Luve

O my luve is like a red, red rose,
    That's newly sprung in June:
O my luve is like the melodie,
    That's sweetly played in tune.

As fair art thou, my bonie lass,
    So deep in luve am I;
And I will luve thee still, my dear,
    Till a' the seas gang dry.

Till a' the seas gang dry, my dear,
    And the rocks melt wi' the sun;
And I will luve thee still, my dear,
    While the sands o' life shall run.

And fare thee weel, my only luve!
    And fare thee weel a while!
And I will come again, my luve,
    Tho' it were ten thousand mile.

ᴇᴠ Robert Burns

Let it be Forgotten

Let it be forgotten, as a flower is forgotten,
    Forgotten as a fire that once was singing gold,
Let it be forgotten for ever and ever,
    Time is a kind friend, he will make us old.

If anyone asks, say it was forgotten
    Long and long ago,
As a flower, as a fire, as a hushed footfall
    In a long-forgotten snow.

SARA TEASDALE

Rosa Canina Burboniana

Originally published as *A Valentine Bouquet*

© 1990 by Barnes & Noble, Inc.
design © 1990 by Charles Ziga
illustrations from *Roses for an Empress*
©1980 by Harenberg Kommunikation, Germany
marbled paper design © 1989 by Ashley Miller
Published by Barnes & Noble Books

ISBN 0-88029-789-1

Acknowledgments

All That's Past, by Walter de la Mare. Reprinted by arrangement with the Literary Trustees of Walter de la Mare and the Society of Authors as th representative.

The Loveliest of Trees, the Cherry Now, by A. E. Housman. © 1939, 1940, 19 by Holt, Rinehart & Winston. Reprinted from *The Collected Poems A. E. Housman*, by permission of Henry Holt & Company.

For Miriam, by Kenneth Patchen. © 1942 by New Directions Publish Corporation. Reprinted by permission of New Directions Publishing.

Let it be Forgotten, by Sara Teasdale. Reprinted by permission of the Macmi Publishing Company, from *The Collected Poems of Sara Teasdale*, © 19 by Macmillan Publishing, renewed 1948 by Mamie T. Wheless.

The Lover Tells of the Rose in his Heart, by W. B. Yeats. Reprinted by arrangem with Macmillan Publishing.

Printed and bound in China

97 98 99 00 01 M 9 8 7 6 5 4 3 2